Emmanuel!

Celebrating God's Presence With Us

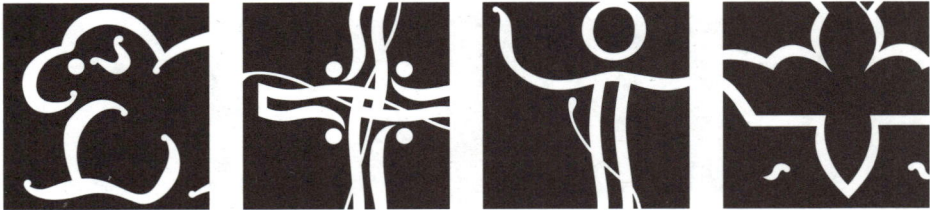

Timothy L. Bias

DISCIPLESHIP RESOURCES

P.O. BOX 840 • NASHVILLE, TENNESSEE 37202-0840

www.discipleshipresources.org

ISBN 0-88177-236-4

Library of Congress Catalog Card No. 97-69411

DR236

Contents

Preface

WHAT REALLY MATTERS IN YOUR LIFE? Look at all the activities that you are involved in. Consider all the dos and don'ts and shoulds and shouldn'ts of your daily life. Ask yourself, Of all these, what really counts? What truly makes a difference in who I am or who I am becoming?

Maybe you have tried religious activities. You have taught Sunday school or been chairperson of the missions committee in a local church. You have participated in worship. You have found the hymns beautiful and the choruses lively. Even the preaching was inspiring at times. But you still feel the void deep within. These religious activities are all nice, but what is the point of doing them? Your prayers seem empty, your goals unreachable, your faith lifeless. The question remains, What really matters? What is at the heart, the center, of your existence?

The apostle Paul wrote to the people at Corinth to tell them about the thing that really mattered to him:

> For I handed on to you as of first importance what I in turn had received: that Christ died for our sins in accordance with the scriptures, and that he was buried, and that he was raised on the third day in accordance with the scriptures. (1 Corinthians 15:3-4)

According to Paul, what really matters—what is of "first importance"—is that Jesus Christ died for our sins, was buried, and was resurrected! For Paul the cross, which is the core of the gospel, is what really counts. The cross is the hinge point that makes a significant difference in all of history. And when the key event of the cross—the crucifixion of Jesus—is connected with the key events of the birth of Jesus, the resurrection of Jesus, and the Spirit of Jesus given at Pentecost, together these events could make an eternal difference in your life.

You are holding in your hand a guide called *Emmanuel! Celebrating God's Presence With Us.* Over the next twenty-eight days, this guide will help you focus on the key events of the life of Jesus Christ. It will also help you focus on what really matters, on what can make a difference in your life and in your community. As you see where God's story and your life story intersect, I hope that you will discover what really matters.

God's story is seen and experienced in God's searching for human beings. The heart of this search is God's coming to be with us and working on our behalf in the person of Jesus Christ. As followers of Jesus Christ, our task is to respond in faith to the event of Jesus Christ, to tell other people about that event, to live in terms of that event, and to invite people to join us in the journey of following Jesus Christ. Responding to the event of Jesus Christ in these ways is the heart of Christian discipleship; it is what really matters.

This guide provides practical ways to enrich your personal journey of following Christ. It challenges you to understand and experience what really counts in the Christian life through remembering, reading, and reflecting. By focusing on the key events in the life of Christ, it provides an opportunity to reflect on how God has come to us humans, has acted on our behalf, and has empowered us to live as Christians in everyday life situations.

Saint Richard of Chichester has captured well the Christian's desire to focus on Jesus:

> O Lord Jesus Christ,...most merciful Redeemer, friend, and brother, may we know thee more clearly, love thee more dearly, and follow thee more nearly.
>
> England, 13th century

I invite you to join me and many others on a journey of focusing on what really matters as we strive to become who God has created us to be.

Let us turn our eyes toward Jesus and journey together.

Timothy L. Bias

How to Use This Guide

EMMANUEL! CELEBRATING GOD'S PRESENCE WITH US is a four-week study guide containing a variety of material for daily prayer, meditation, and action. The guide can be used by individuals for personal devotional study, or in group settings, such as Sunday school classes, study groups, ministry teams, and committees in the congregation, or study groups meeting in homes.

The daily Scripture readings, prayers, readings for reflection, and suggestions for action are grouped under a theme for each of the four weeks of the study. These themes focus on the key events in the life of Christ: birth, crucifixion, resurrection, and the giving of the Spirit at Pentecost. The guide is structured in a way that allows people to read about and reflect upon the key events in the life of Christ and how these events shape Christian faith. It also encourages readers to find ways to live out their insights from the study in their daily lives. By engaging both thinking and doing, *Emmanuel!* provides an arena for making, sustaining, and deploying faithful disciples of Jesus Christ.

As you prepare to begin the study, look over the following explanation of the weekly meditations for reflection and action. The components and structure of these meditations are the same for each of the four weeks:

Introduction: This section introduces the key event for the week and presents some assumptions and thoughts about the key event that may guide your meditation for the week. Read the Introduction at the beginning of the week, and again at the end of the week to review what you have learned and experienced.

Opening Prayer: This prayer invites you to enter into the presence of the Lord believing that the Lord is waiting to meet us. The Opening Prayer focuses on Christ and relates to the key event of the week. Read the prayer every day as you begin your study.

Scripture Readings: The seven Scripture readings are intended to support the key event for the week. Each day, read the designated Scripture passage carefully; look for a truth to guide your life that day. To benefit most from the Scripture reading, study the passage with an open mind and heart; savor every word. Be aware of how the Scripture relates to your own history, actions, and desires. Engage the Scripture passage with your heart, your mind, and your emotions. Read the passage as if it were written just for you. Look for images or phrases in the passage that may help you enter into dialogue with God. As you reflect upon the Scripture, write your thoughts and feelings on the page titled "Your Thoughts for the Week," found at the end of each chapter. If you are using this guide as part of a group, share your notes and insights with group members when you meet.

Prayer of Formation: After reflecting on the day's Scripture passage, pray this prayer to allow God to form you into God's image. The Prayer of Formation helps you examine your life before God and provides direction for how to live faithfully as Christ's disciple every day. Pray this prayer every day of the four-week period.

Readings for Reflection: When you have finished the Prayer of Formation, read one or more selections from the Readings for Reflection. The readings were selected to provide you with a variety of ways to reflect upon the key event of the week. As you reflect on each reading, look for ways to help you experience the events of the life of Christ in everyday living. Write your thoughts and feelings on the "Your Thoughts for the Week" page at the end of the chapter.

Please note that because the readings are quotations, some may contain gender-exclusive language. Try to focus on the message of the readings and their relevance to the key events. Words in brackets indicate the author's remarks.

Suggestions for Reflection and Action: This section asks questions to guide your reflection and action every day. Use the questions each day to help you write your thoughts, feelings, insights, and prayer concerns on the page titled "Your Thoughts for the Week" at the end of the chapter. Be honest in your writing. Write for yourself and God alone. This is a personal record of your journey with God. Recording your walk with God honestly will help you reflect on the events, joys, and challenges of your life. It will also help you discover where God is leading you through those situations and circumstances.

If you are using this guide as part of a group, you will be encouraged to share with the group some thoughts and insights from your reflection on the Scripture readings, the prayers, the readings for reflection, and your own experience. Since these notes reflect your own journey with God, you may decide that some of them are too personal to share with the group. Prayerfully select the thoughts and insights that you think will strengthen group discussion.

Closing Prayer: This prayer helps you close your study time. It also sends you forth into ministry for the day. As you conclude your time of study, prayer, and reflection, remember that God is sending you into a mission field—the world in which you live, work, and play every day—to follow Christ and to invite others to join you in following Christ.

As you begin this study of the life of Christ, may you experience the blessing of God every day.

The Birth of Jesus

INTRODUCTION

DURING THE CIVIL WAR, the Union and Confederate armies were locked in a vicious battle just outside the city of Richmond, Virginia. As night fell after the first day of the battle, cheers rang out from the Confederate line. When General Grant asked what was going on behind the enemy's line, he was told that General George Pickett's troops were celebrating because they had just received word that Pickett's wife had given birth to a baby boy.

Upon receiving the news, General Grant gave orders for bonfires to be lit and a toast to be given. Cheers and hurrahs rang out all night long. For a few hours, the shooting stopped and enemies were drawn together. The birth of Pickett's son had made a difference in the lives of soldiers on both sides of the battle line. Just as the birth of Pickett's son made a difference to enemies locked in combat, so the birth of God's Son makes a difference in the lives of people today. When Jesus Christ is born in our lives, our lives change.

One of the key events in Christianity is the birth of God's Son, Jesus Christ. In Jesus Christ, God took on the life of a human being and came into this world to live with humanity. We call this action on God's part the Incarnation. The word *incarnation* means "to become flesh." The birth of Jesus in a stable to humble parents named Mary and Joseph was God's dramatic means of coming into the world in such a way that we can understand who God is.

God always comes to us in a way that satisfies our need for God at those times when we need God most. Matthew reminds us in his Gospel that the name *Jesus* means savior, and that the name *Emmanuel* means God is with us. Matthew is telling us that in Jesus, God's saving love is with us.

Luke reminds us in his Gospel that Jesus identified with outcasts and second-class citizens. Jesus was born in a stable because there was no "respect-able" place available. His birth was announced to shepherds, who were consid-ered unclean and unacceptable in good religious circles. Luke is telling us that God's saving love is for everyone.

John reminds us in his Gospel that Christ was present in the beginning *with* God because Christ *is* God. Then God became flesh and lived among us in Jesus Christ. I understand the words *lived among us* to mean "pitched his tent next to ours." John is telling us that God in Jesus has come to live with us.

Paul reminds us in his letters that God in Christ "was reconciling the world to himself" (2 Corinthians 5:19). It might be helpful to think of the word *recon-ciled* as meaning embraced or hugged. God in Christ was "hugging" the world to himself.

In other words, God has come to you in Jesus Christ on your turf to embrace you with love. The good news of the Incarnation is that no matter who you are or what you have done, God has come to be with you. God has come to embrace you and to hold you in redeeming, transforming, and encouraging love.

The key event of the Incarnation is both a window and a mirror. It is a win-dow through which we are allowed to catch a glimpse of God's nature. The apostle Paul expressed what he saw through the window: Out of the magni-tude of the divine love (Romans 8:38-39) God sent God's Son in human flesh (Romans 8:3), reconciling the world unto God's self (2 Corinthians 5:19). What an indescribable gift (2 Corinthians 9:15)! When we catch a glimpse of such an act of love and generosity, there is nothing left for us to do but live our lives in grateful adoration.

The Incarnation is also a mirror in which we see God reflected in human nature. What does that reflection look like? The answer is, it looks like Jesus Christ.

Jesus was touchable, approachable, reachable, ordinary. In fact, were the historical Jesus to appear in flesh and blood today, you probably wouldn't notice him as he walked through the shopping mall. He wouldn't turn heads by the clothes he wore or the jewelry he flashed. He would watch television at your house, wrestle with your kids, doze on your couch, and cook steaks on your grill. He'd laugh at your jokes and tell a few of his own. When you spoke, he'd listen. But do not forget: Jesus *is* among us today. In the power of the Holy Spirit, the resurrected Jesus is as close as the joys and hurts of your next-door neighbor, the grocery clerk, the kids on the street.

If it is true that God came to be with us in Jesus Christ, is it not also true that God will meet us in the circumstances of the people with whom we live, work, and associate? Where will you meet Jesus this week? Will you meet him at the grocery store, at the office, on the street, on the playground? Will you meet him on the golf course, at the spa, at the club?

As you begin Week One of the study, think of the places in your community where you might meet God, and where the Word might become flesh in your everyday living.

• Opening Prayer •

(Pray this prayer every day as a way to begin your time with God.)

O living and loving God, who came to this world long ago in the birth of Jesus Christ, be born in me anew today by the power of your Holy Spirit. I offer my life as a home to you and ask for grace and strength to live as your faithful, joyful child today and every day. I offer myself to you in and through your Son and my Lord, Jesus Christ. Amen.

• Scripture Readings •

(Read the Scripture for the day slowly and meditatively.)

Day 1	Matthew 1:18-25	**Day 5**	Galatians 4:4-7
Day 2	Matthew 2:1-11	**Day 6**	John 1:1-18
Day 3	Luke 2:1-7	**Day 7**	2 Corinthians 5:16-21
Day 4	Luke 2:8-20		

• Prayer of Formation •

(Pray this prayer to examine your life before God and to be formed in the faith. Pray the prayer below, then add to it your thanks to God for this day and for family and friends. Pray for your church family. If you are using this guide as part of a group, pray for the other participants. After the prayer, proceed to Readings for Reflection.)

> Lord, make me an instrument of thy peace;
> where there is hatred, let me sow love;
> where there is injury, pardon;

where there is doubt, faith;
where there is despair, hope;
where there is darkness, light;
and where there is sadness, joy.

O Divine Master,
grant that I may not so much seek
to be consoled as to console;
to be understood, as to understand;
to be loved, as to love;
for it is in giving that we receive,
it is in pardoning that we are pardoned,
and it is in dying that we are born to eternal life.

Francis of Assisi, Italy, 13th century

• Readings for Reflection •

(Read one or more of the following readings prayerfully each day. As you meditate, look for connections among the readings, the Scripture passage for the day, and the prayers.)

Come, thou long-expected Jesus,
born to set thy people free;
from our fears and sins release us,
let us find our rest in thee.
Israel's strength and consolation,
hope of all the earth thou art;
dear desire of every nation,
joy of every longing heart.

Born thy people to deliver,
born a child and yet a King,
born to reign in us forever,
now thy gracious kingdom bring.
By thine own eternal spirit
rule in all our hearts alone;
by thine all sufficient merit,
raise us to thy glorious throne.

—Charles Wesley, "Come, Thou Long-Expected Jesus"

It's Christmas night....For a few precious hours, he is beheld. Christ the Lord. Those who pass the year without seeing him, suddenly see him. People who have been accustomed to using his name in vain, pause to use it in praise. Eyes, now free of the blinders of self, marvel at his majesty.

All of a sudden he's everywhere.

In the grin of the policeman as he drives the paddy wagon full of presents to the orphanage.

In the twinkle in the eyes of the Taiwanese waiter as he tells of his upcoming Christmas trip to see his children.

In the emotion of the father who is too thankful to finish the dinner table prayer.

He's in the tears of the mother as she welcomes home her son from overseas.

He's in the heart of the man who spent Christmas morning on skid row giving away cold baloney sandwiches and warm wishes.

And he's in the solemn silence of the crowd of shopping mall shoppers as the elementary school chorus sings "Away in a Manger."

Emmanuel. He is with us.

—Max Lucado, *God Came Near*

Emmanuel, Emmanuel,
his name is called Emmanuel.
God with us, revealed in us,
his name is called Emmanuel.

—Bob McGee, "Emmanuel, Emmanuel"

A ship is at sea, and a man is overboard. He is going down for the third and final time. One can see a hand extended above the surface of the water. There are certain individuals standing along the railing of the ship, giving the floundering man advice.

First, there is a "moralist." He looks out, sees the poor man's dilemma, reaches into his attaché case and pulls out a book on how to be a good swimmer. He tosses it to him saying, "Here, read this and follow the rules, and you will be okay."

Then, there is an "idealist." He sees the terrible plight of the drowning man, jumps into the water, swims up beside him and says, "Now you watch me and do exactly as I!"

Then, there is a man that we could call a "representative of the institutional church." He sees the man and yells out, "Just hold on brother, we'll call a committee meeting and dialogue your dilemma. If funds are sufficient, we will appoint another committee and they will engage in the act of rescuing you!"

There is another man who represents the school of "positive thought." His heart aches as he sees the man drowning and he yells out: "You're not really drowning at all, it's just in your head! Think dry! You'll be okay!"

There is another whom we call a "traditional revivalist." He is imprisoned by outworn ideas and stereotyped methodology. He sees a hand extended above the surface of the water and adopts a kind of sacred shakiness in his voice. He says, "Yes, I see that hand; are there others?"

Finally, there is a "realist" on board. He sees the plight of the drowning man, rips off his outer garments, kicks off his shoes, grabs a lifesaver with rope attached, and leaps into the icy water. He swims up, grabs the man, and engages in the act of rescuing him at the risk of his own life.

This is what God has done through his Son, Jesus Christ. He was not, and is not, unwilling to identify himself with our plight. He entered into life and felt the pulsebeat of society. He knew our heartaches and our sorrows. He knew what it was like to be scorned, rejected, beaten, and even put to death. He experienced life at the point where men sweat and smell, bleed and die.

—George E. Morris, *Imperatives for Evangelism*

© Tidings, Nashville, TN.

When God chose to reveal himself to mankind, what medium did he use? A book? No, that was secondary. A church? No. That was consequential. A moral code? No. To limit God's revelation to a cold list of do's and don'ts is as tragic as looking at a Colorado road-map and saying that you'd seen the Rockies.

When God chose to reveal himself, he did so (surprise of surprises) through a human body. The tongue that called forth the dead was a human one. The hand that touched the leper had dirt under its nails. The feet upon which the woman wept were calloused and dusty. And his tears...oh, don't miss the tears ...they came from a heart as broken as yours or mine ever has been.

—Max Lucado, *God Came Near*

I spent five years as a pastor in Gulfport, Mississippi. Though not an ardent fisherman, I fished enough to observe an interesting phenomenon that became a parable for Christ, "the image of the invisible God" as Paul calls him in Colossians 1.

Near the Bay of Biloxi in the Mississippi Sound, the level of the bayous changes with the high and low tides. These bayous feed the ocean, emptying their waters into the larger body at low tide. At high tide, the ocean feeds the bayous, raising their level. To the fisherman, there is significance other than the tide. Up the bayous for a certain distance, the water is brackish, flavored by the salt of the Gulf waters. White and speckled trout, whose natural habitat is the Gulf, are bountiful in this brackish water. But further inland, the waters lose their salt content, and freshwater fish such as green and rainbow trout hover in the cool depths.

The analogy is this: ...The bayous go to the ocean, but the ocean also comes to the bayous. Though limited, as all our words and parables are, it's a faint effort to picture Christ. Christ shows us what God is; he also shows us what all persons are meant to be. "Found in the fashion of man," he was human, revealing the model of our humanity—the image in which we were created. But also in him, the ocean of God has come to us. [So Christ is a window through which we see the very nature of God, and a mirror revealing our human possibility by picturing our fallen state and the fallen state of all life against the image of our divine destiny.]

—Maxie Dunnam, *This Is Christianity*

[Jesus said, "For truly I tell you, whoever gives you a cup of water to drink because you bear the name of Christ will by no means lose the reward" (Mark 9:41). When we do good things to others, we do good things to God.

"And the king will answer them, 'Truly I tell you, just as you did it to one of the least of these who are members of my family, you did it to me'" (Matthew 25:40).]

Make an investment in the people the world has cast off—the homeless, the AIDS patient, the orphan, the divorcee—and you may discover the source of your independence.

Jesus' message is stirring: "The way you treat them is the way you treat me."

...The person who sees Christ is the one who sees the hurting person. To see Jesus, go to the convalescent home, sit down beside the elderly woman, and steady her hand as she puts the spoon in her mouth. To see Jesus, go to the community hospital and ask the nurse to take you to see one who has received no visits. To see Jesus, leave your office and go down the hall and talk to the man who is regretting his divorce and missing his children. To see Jesus, go to the inner city and give a sandwich—not a sermon, but a sandwich—to the bag lady who's made a home out of an overpass.

To see Jesus...see the unattractive and forgotten.

—Max Lucado, *And the Angels Were Silent*

One evening I went to eat at a restaurant in Port-au-Prince, Haiti. I sat down at a table in the front of the restaurant, next to the window. I ordered my food and it was quickly served. Then, just as I was about to plunge the fork into the food, I looked to my right and discovered four little Haitian boys standing there on the other side of the window. With their noses pressed flat against the glass, they were staring at my food. They did not even seem to notice me. Instead, their eyes were riveted on the food on my plate. They were dirty, almost naked children—some of the hundreds who wander the streets of Port-au-Prince, belonging to no one, and for whom no one cares. They were the throw-away-children of an impoverished society and would probably be dead within a few years. (Almost half of the children born in Haiti die before the age of twelve.)

I was frozen in upset. Before I could react, the waiter saw my predicament. He quickly came back to my table and pulled down the window shade. Then he said, "Don't let them bother you, sir. Don't let them bother you. Enjoy your meal." As if it would have been possible to have enjoyed my meal after having seen those desperate children! However, don't we all do what that waiter did? Don't we all pull down the shade? Don't we all close out the hungry people of the world?

There are millions of them out there. Millions of incarnations of the resurrected Jesus, and they are suffering from malnutrition and dying from diseases that they have no strength to resist. They live without hope. They live without help. But in the face of these realities, we go on living our affluent lives. We eat our meals, drink our milk and have our desserts while, concealed from our eyes, they writhe in desperate suffering.

—Anthony Campolo, *It's Friday, but Sunday's Comin'*

Christ has
No body now on earth but yours;
No hands but yours;
No feet but yours;
Yours are the eyes
Through which is to look out
Christ's compassion to the world;
Yours are the feet
With which he is to go about
Doing good;
Yours are the hands
With which he is to bless now.

—St. Teresa of Avila, 16th century

Some years ago I was doing missionary work in Haiti and in the Dominican Republic. One afternoon, near the border separating those two countries, I stood on the edge of a grass landing strip waiting for a small Piper Cub airplane to come to pick me up and fly me back to the capital city. As I stood there, a woman came toward me. In her hands she was holding her baby. The child's stomach was swelled to four or five times normal size because of malnutrition. The arms and legs of the little boy were so spindly that they appeared to be nothing more than bones covered with skin. He was a black child but his hair had taken on the rust color that evidences a lack of protein. The child's mouth was hanging open, and his eyes were rolled back so that they appeared to be white bulges in his skull. The baby was dirty and filthy and obviously close to death. The woman held the child up to me and then began pleading for me to take her child. "Please, mister, please take my baby; take my baby with you," she begged. "Take my baby to your country. Feed my baby. Take care of my baby. Don't let my baby die."

I didn't know what to do. I couldn't take her baby. There were hundreds of babies like this in the surrounding countryside. What could I do in the face of such overpowering suffering? I pushed her away and I told her, "I can't help you. I can't take your baby. Do you understand? There's nothing I can do!"

She pleaded again, "Mister, don't let my baby die. Please, mister, don't let my baby die. Take my baby. Please take my baby with you."

Again I pushed her aside but she kept on pleading with me....

I was relieved when I saw the Piper Cub airplane come into sight and touch down at the edge of the grass landing strip. As it rolled toward me I ran out to meet it. I wanted to get away from that woman and her baby. But she came running after me. She was screaming at the top of her lungs, "Take my baby! Take my baby! Don't let my baby die!" She was hysterical in her pleading as I climbed into the airplane and closed the Plexiglas door. Before the pilot could turn the airplane around for the takeoff, she was alongside us, banging the fuselage of the airplane and screaming at me, "Don't let my baby die! Don't let my baby die!"

The engine revved up. The pilot released the brakes of the plane and we began to move away from the woman and down the landing strip. She ran alongside the plane, still clutching her horribly emaciated baby and screaming at me to take her child. At last the plane lifted into the air, and as we soared into the sky, the pilot banked so that we turned and flew back over the landing field. As we did so, I got one last look at that woman who by then was standing motionless in the middle of the landing strip clutching her baby. We flew away and I tried to put that woman and her baby out of my mind. But I couldn't. Halfway back to the capital it hit me. It dawned on me who that baby was. I realized who it was that I had left behind on that landing strip. The name of that child was Jesus. Regardless of the name his parents had given him at birth, I knew that his name was Jesus. It was Jesus who was incarnated in the feeble, sickly frame. It was Jesus who had been held out to me for love and care. It was Jesus whom I had shut out of my life.

—Anthony Campolo, *It's Friday, but Sunday's Comin'*

Oswald Goulter was a missionary in China for thirty-two years. The last three years of his ministry there, he was imprisoned under house arrest. Finally, mid-December 1949, he was released. The missionary organization that had assigned him sent him money to return home. He made his way to India, where he was to catch a ship home to the United States. It was while he was there that he heard of shiploads of Jews who had not been welcomed into any country in the world. Only in India were they allowed ashore temporarily. There they were living in barn lofts and attics.

Dr. Goulter went to them and said, "Merry Christmas!"

They said, "We're Jews."

Again he said, "Merry Christmas!"

And again they replied, "We don't keep Christmas. We're Jews."

He said, "But it's Christmas. What would you like for Christmas?"

They responded, "We told you! We're Jews."

He asked again, "What would you like for Christmas?"

He kept on and on until finally they melted and said, "Some German pastry."

Dr. Goulter cashed in his ticket for the trip home, bought boxes of German pastry, and took it to the attics and barn lofts. "Merry Christmas!" he said, "Merry Christmas!"

That story was told several years later on an occasion when Dr. Goulter was present. Dr. Goulter was 86 or 87 years old at the time. Someone looked at him and asked, "Dr. Goulter, did you really do that?"

Dr. Goulter laughed and said, "Yes. Yes."

A young theological student in the group who was right about most things stood and almost shouted, "I can't believe you did that!"

Dr. Goulter replied, "Well, I did. Was it wrong? Did I do something wrong?"

The student said, "How could you do that? Those people don't even believe in Jesus."

Dr. Goulter replied, "But I do."

—Fred B. Craddock, sermon excerpt

Used by permission.

I try to give to the poor people for love what the rich could get for money. No, I wouldn't touch a leper for a thousand pounds; yet I willingly cure him for the love of God.

—Mother Teresa of Calcutta, *A Gift for God: Prayers and Meditations*

A Gift for God, by Mother Teresa, copyright © 1975 by Mother Teresa Missionaries of Charity. Used by permission of HarperCollins Publishers, Inc.

• Suggestions for Reflection and Action •

(As you read, pray, and reflect each day, write your thoughts, feelings, and reflections under "Your Thoughts for the Week," page 21. The questions below may help focus your meditation.)

- What is God saying to me through the Scripture reading, prayers, and readings for reflection?
- Where is God present in the community?
- Where do I experience God in the places where I live, work, and play?
- How can God be present to others through me?
- How can God be present to the community through my congregation?
- What one action of faithful discipleship am I going to take today?

• Closing Prayer •

(Pray this prayer to close your time with God.)

O God, help me to be aware of your presence in every situation I am in today. Give me ears to hear what you are saying. Give me a heart and mind to discern and understand what you are doing. Make me a blessing to someone somewhere today. Amen.

• Your Thoughts for the Week •

(Use this page as a personal record of your journey with God. Write your thoughts, feelings, insights, and prayer concerns daily as you reflect on the Scripture reading, prayers, readings for reflection, Suggestions for Reflection and Action questions, and your own daily living.)

The Crucifixion of Jesus

INTRODUCTION

AS I SAID in the Preface, the key event of the cross is truly the core of the Christian gospel. However, we often find it hard to fathom God's great love for us in the death of Jesus. Perhaps the following story about human love will provide a modest clue to the depths of the divine love:

> A woman came to see [a plastic surgeon], Dr. [Maxwell] Maltz, one day about her husband. She told the doctor that her husband had been injured in a fire while attempting to save his parents from a burning house. He couldn't get to them. They both were killed, and his face was burned and disfigured. He had given up on life and gone into hiding. He wouldn't let anyone see him—not even his wife.
>
> Dr. Maltz told the woman not to worry. "With the great advances we've made in plastic surgery in recent years," he said, "I can restore his face."
>
> She explained that he wouldn't let anyone help him because he believed God disfigured his face to punish him for not saving his parents.
>
> Then she made a shocking request: "I want you to disfigure my face so I can be like him! If I can share in his pain, then maybe he will let me back into his life. I

love him so much, I want to be with him. And if that is what it takes, then that is what I want to do."

Of course, Dr. Maltz would not agree, but he was moved deeply by that wife's determined and total love. He got her permission to try to talk to her husband. He went to the man's room and knocked, but there was no answer. He called loudly through the door, "I know you are in there and I know you can hear me, so I've come to tell you that my name is Dr. Maxwell Maltz. I'm a plastic surgeon, and I want you to know that I can restore your face."

There was no response. Again he called loudly, "Please come out and let me help restore your face." But again there was no answer. Still speaking through the door, Dr. Maltz told the man what his wife was asking him to do. "She wants me to disfigure her face, to make her face like yours in the hope that you will let her back into your life. That's how much she loves you. That's how much she wants to help you!"

There was a brief moment of silence, and then ever so slowly, the doorknob began to turn. The disfigured man came out to make a new beginning and to find a new life. He was set free, brought out of hiding, given a new start by his wife's love.

It's a dramatic expression of human love that gives us a picture, however faint, of the saving love of Jesus Christ.

From *This Is Christianity*, by Maxie Dunnam, pages 60–61.
Copyright © 1994 by Abingdon Press. Used by permission.

God has come not only to be *with* us in this world but to be *for* us. As the apostle Paul put it, God is for us by not sparing God's own Son but giving him up out of love for us all (Romans 8:31-32).

No matter who you are or what you have done, God loves you. There is nothing you can do to keep God from loving you. God has *chosen* to love you, and there is nothing you can do about the matter—nothing but accept that love.

"But God proves his love for us in that while we were still sinners Christ died for us" (Romans 5:8). This Scripture changed my life. I realized that Christ died for me not after I repented, not after I asked for forgiveness, not after I asked for acceptance, not after I got "all my ducks in a row." Christ died for me long before I made a response to his love. Christ died for me while I still had no understanding of what it meant to be a Christian and a follower of Jesus Christ. Christ died for me while I was professing that I believed in Jesus Christ but was living as if he made no difference at all.

Jesus was not crucified between two candlesticks in a church sanctuary. He was crucified between two thieves on a garbage heap in the midst of failure and disgust, blood and discouragement.

Remember, God knows your aches. God knows your loneliness. God knows your emptiness, anger, frustration, and separation. God knows the tragedy, the hopelessness, the fear, and the pain. God also knows your joys, your love, your goodness, and your celebrations. In the midst of it all, God has come to be *with* you and *for* you in Jesus Christ.

That is why when you experience God's love, you want to share that love with others. Where will you meet Jesus this week? Will you meet him while listening to the hurts and frustrations of your spouse? Will you meet him while forgiving a colleague or an enemy? Will you meet him while looking into the eyes of a child who wants love and acceptance? Because God is with us and for us in Jesus Christ, how can you be with and for others in the places where you live, work, and play this week?

As you start the second week of this study, think of the places in your community where you might meet God and where you can be with and for broken and hurting people every day.

• Opening Prayer •

(Pray this prayer every day as a way to begin your time with God.)

Almighty God, you are the light and life of every soul and my only source of hope. In this time of prayer and reflection, help me experience your transforming power that prepares me for ministry this day. I offer this time to you in the name of Jesus Christ, my Lord and Savior. Amen.

• Scripture Readings •

(Read the Scripture for the day slowly and meditatively.)

Day 1 Matthew 26:1–27:66   **Day 5** Isaiah 53:1-9
Day 2 Mark 14:1–15:47   **Day 6** Philippians 2:1-13
Day 3 Luke 22:1–23:56   **Day 7** 1 Corinthians 1:18-25
Day 4 John 18:1–19:42

• Prayer of Formation •

(Pray this prayer to examine your life before God and to be formed in the faith. Pray the prayer below, then add to it your thanks to God for this day and for family and friends. Pray for your church family. If you are using this guide as part of a group, pray for the other participants. After the prayer, proceed to Readings for Reflection.)

> Lord, make me an instrument of thy peace;
> where there is hatred, let me sow love;
> where there is injury, pardon;

where there is doubt, faith;
where there is despair, hope;
where there is darkness, light;
and where there is sadness, joy.

O Divine Master,
grant that I may not so much seek
to be consoled as to console;
to be understood, as to understand;
to be loved, as to love;
for it is in giving that we receive,
it is in pardoning that we are pardoned,
and it is in dying that we are born to eternal life.

Francis of Assisi, Italy, 13th century

• Readings for Reflection •

(Read one or more of the following readings prayerfully each day. As you meditate, look for connections among the readings, the Scripture passage for the day, and the prayers.)

When I survey the wondrous cross
on which the Prince of Glory died,
my richest gain I count but loss
and pour contempt on all my pride.

Forbid it, Lord, that I should boast,
save in the death of Christ, my God;
all the vain things that charm me most,
I sacrifice them to his blood.

See, from his head, his hands, his feet,
sorrow and love flow mingled down.
Did e'er such love and sorrow meet,
or thorns compose so rich a crown?

Were the whole realm of nature mine,
that were an offering far too small;
love so amazing, so divine,
demands my soul, my life, my all.

—Isaac Watts, "When I Survey the Wondrous Cross"

In the evening I went very unwillingly to a society in Aldersgate-Street, where one was reading Luther's preface to the Epistle to the Romans. About a quarter before nine, while he was describing the change which God works in the heart through faith in Christ, I felt my heart strangely warmed. I felt I did trust in Christ, Christ alone for salvation: And an assurance was given me, that he had taken away my sins, even mine, and saved me from the law of sin and death.

—John Wesley, *The Works of John Wesley, Volume One*

O Love divine, what hast thou done!
The immortal God hath died for me!
The Father's co-eternal Son
bore all my sins upon the tree.
Th'immortal God for me hath died:
My Lord, my Love, is crucified!

Is crucified for me and you,
to bring us rebels back to God.
Believe, believe the record true,
ye all are bought with Jesus' blood.
Pardon for all flows from his side:
My Lord, my Love, is crucified!

Behold him, all ye that pass by,
the bleeding Prince of life and peace!
Come, sinners, see your Savior die,
and say, "Was ever grief like his?"
Come, feel with me his blood applied:
My Lord, my Love, is crucified!

—Charles Wesley, "O Love Divine, What Hast Thou Done"

We are not happy because we are unforgiving, and we are unforgiving because we feel superior to others.

Mercy is the fruit of the highest degree of love, because love creates equals, and a greater love makes us inferior.

First let us establish three premises:

Those who do not love feel superior to everyone else.

Those who love feel equal to everyone else.

Those who love much gladly take the lower place.

Each one of us can identify his position somewhere along this spectrum, which comprises the three degrees of the spiritual life here on earth:

Death for those who do not love.

Life for those who love.

Holiness for those who love much.

The beatitude of the merciful relates, like all the beatitudes, to the realm of holiness and we have to admit that Jesus set his sights high when he had the courage and confidence to place this lofty ideal before us. It is the beatitude that he himself lived to the full, stooping, out of love, to the lowest place, even to the extent of being rejected as a common criminal, fit only to be hung on a gibbet [cross].

—Carlo Carretto, *In Search of the Beyond*

Taken from *In Search of the Beyond*, by Carlo Carretto. Published by Orbis Books, Maryknoll, New York, and copyright 1975 by Darton, Longman and Todd, Ltd. Used by permission of the publishers.

Turn your eyes upon Jesus,
look full in his wonderful face,
and the things of earth will grow strangely dim
in the light of his glory and grace.

—Helen H. Lemmel, from "Turn Your Eyes Upon Jesus"

During the Vietnam conflict, a young graduate of West Point Academy was sent to Vietnam to lead a group of new recruits into battle. He did his job well, trying his best to keep his men from ambush and death. However, one night he and his men were overtaken by a battalion of the Viet Cong. He was able to get all but one of his men to safety. The one soldier who had been left behind had been severely wounded, and from their trenches, the young lieutenant and his men could hear their wounded comrade moaning and crying for help. They all knew that venturing out into the vicious crossfire of the enemy would mean almost certain death. But the groanings of the wounded soldier continued on through the night. Eventually, the endurance of the young lieutenant came to an end, and he crawled out of his place of safety toward the cries of the dying man. He got to him safely and was able to drag him back. But just as he pushed the wounded man into the safety of the trench, he himself caught a bullet in the back and was killed instantly.

Several months later, the rescued man returned to the United States, and when the parents of the dead hero heard that he was in their vicinity, they planned to have him come to dinner. They wanted to know this young man whose life was spared at such a great cost to them.

On the night of the dinner party, their guest arrived drunk. He was loud and boisterous. He told off-color jokes and showed no concern for his suffering hosts. The parents of the dead hero did the best they could to make it a worthwhile evening, but their efforts went unrewarded.

At the end of that torturous visit, the obscene guest left. As her husband closed the door, the mother collapsed in tears and cried, "To think that our precious son had to die for somebody like that."

—Tony Campolo, *Who Switched the Price Tags?*

From heav'n You came, helpless Babe,
Enter'd our world, Your glory veiled;
Not to be served, but to serve,
And give Your life that we might live.

There in the garden of tears,
My heavy load He chose to bear;
His heart with sorrow was torn,
"Yet not My will, but Yours," He said.

Come, see His hands and His feet,
The scars that speak of sacrifice;
Hands that flung stars into space,
To cruel nails surrendered.

So let us learn how to serve,
And in our lives enthrone Him;
Each other's needs to prefer,
For it is Christ we're serving.

Refrain:
This is our God, the Servant King,
He calls us now to follow Him;
To bring our lives as a daily offering
Of worship to the Servant King.

—Graham Kendrick, "From Heaven You Came (The Servant King)"

God is not stumped by an evil world. He doesn't gasp in amazement at the dearth of our faith or the depth of our failures. We can't surprise God with our cruelties. He knows the condition of the world...and loves it just the same. For just when we find a place where God would never be..., we look again and there he is, in the flesh.

—Max Lucado, *No Wonder They Call Him the Savior*

✝

[Harry Denman] was speaking at a series of meetings at City Temple in London for Dr. Leslie Weatherhead. While in his office one day, a call came from a rundown rooming house. A prostitute who was dying had asked for a Methodist minister. The pastor asked Dr. Denman to go with him. When they arrived he asked Dr. Denman to minister to the dying woman.

Dr. Denman knelt down beside her bed, bowed his head, and prayed silently. When he finished he held the woman's hand and said to her, using her first name, which he had learned beforehand, "Mary, Papa just told me to tell you that He loves you and wants you to come home to Him." She smiled and died at that moment.

—A.J. Schrader, *Prophetic Evangelist*

✝

I cast all my cares upon You.
I lay all of my burdens down at Your feet.
And any time that I don't know what to do,
I will cast all my cares upon You.

—Kelly Willard, from "Cares Chorus"

✝

A friend of mine was on a train traveling out of Victoria Station in London. Across from him in the compartment were two men in their early thirties. Twenty minutes out of the station, one of them had an epileptic seizure.

Perhaps you know how frightening such a seizure can be. The man stiffened and fell heavily out of his seat. Immediately, his friend took off his own jacket, rolled it up and put it behind his friend's head. He blotted the beads of perspiration from his brow with his handkerchief, talked to the stricken man in a quiet manner and calmed him. When the seizure was over, he lifted his friend gently back into his seat.

Then he turned to my friend and said, "Mister, please forgive us. Sometimes this happens two or three times a day. My buddy and I were in Vietnam together, and we were both wounded. I had bullets in both my legs and he had one in his shoulder. The helicopter that was supposed to come for us never came to pick us up.

"My friend picked me up, mister, and he carried me for three and one half days out of that jungle. The Viet Cong were sniping at us the whole way. He was in more agony than I was. I begged him to drop me and save himself, but he wouldn't let me go. He got me out of that jungle, mister. He saved my life. I don't know how he did it and I don't know why he did it.

"Four years ago, I found out that he had this condition, so I sold my house in New York, took what money I had, and came over here to take care of him." And then he looked at his friend and said, "You see, mister, after what he did for me, there isn't anything I wouldn't do for him."

—Tony Campolo, *You Can Make a Difference*

You Can Make a Difference, Tony Campolo, © 1984 Word Publishers, Nashville, TN. All rights reserved.

God forgave my sin in Jesus' name,
I've been born again in Jesus' name,
and in Jesus' name I come to you,
to share his love as he told me to.

All power is given in Jesus' name,
in earth and heaven in Jesus' name,
and in Jesus' name I come to you,
to share his power as he told me to.

Refrain:
He said, "Freely, freely you have received,
freely, freely give.
Go in my name, and because you believe,
others will know that I live."

—Carol Owens, "Freely, Freely"

• Suggestions for Reflection and Action •

(As you read, pray, and reflect each day, write your thoughts, feelings, and reflections under "Your Thoughts for the Week," page 33. The questions below may help focus your meditation.)

- What is God saying to me through the Scripture reading, prayers, and readings for reflection?
- Where are people hurting in the community?
- Where do I experience God in the places where I live, work, and play?
- How can God be present to others through me?
- How can God be present to the community through my congregation?
- What one action of faithful discipleship am I going to take today?

• Closing Prayer •

(Pray this prayer to close your time with God.)

O God, help me to be aware of your presence in every situation I am in today. Give me ears to hear what you are saying. Give me a heart and mind to discern and understand what you are doing in the world. Make me a blessing to someone today. Amen.

• Your Thoughts for the Week •

(Use this page as a personal record of your journey with God. Write your thoughts, feelings, insights, and prayer concerns daily as you reflect on the Scripture reading, prayers, readings for reflection, Suggestions for Reflection and Action questions, and your own daily living.)

Emmanuel!

The Resurrection of Jesus

INTRODUCTION

THE CRUCIFIXION OF JESUS cannot—and must not—be separated from his resurrection. As the Gospel accounts of the Resurrection show, Jesus never foretold his death without foretelling his rising again. He never thought of the shame without the triumph. The humiliation and the glory were inseparably connected. One could not exist without the other.

The attention of the early church was focused on the Resurrection. In Simon Peter's address to the people in the Temple, he said,

> The God of Abraham, the God of Isaac, and the God of Jacob, the God of our ancestors has glorified his servant Jesus, whom you handed over and rejected in the presence of Pilate, though he had decided to release him. But you rejected the Holy and Righteous One and asked to have a murderer given to you, and you killed the Author of life, whom God raised from the dead. To this we are witnesses. (Acts 3:13-15)

The heart of the preaching of Jesus' earliest followers was that God had raised Jesus from the dead. These followers of the risen Christ saw themselves as evidence of the power of the Resurrection to transform lives.

However, as Acts 3:13-15 also shows, when Jesus lived and worked among us, we found his presence uncomfortable. Indeed, we felt compelled to do away with him. So we nailed Jesus to a cross and said in effect:

> You go back home, God. Don't you mess around down here. We have to watch our language too much with you around. And we have to watch our ledger accounts too much when you're looking over our shoulder....God, you go back home...where you belong and be a good God, and we'll see you at eleven o'clock on Sunday morning.
>
> From *The Substance of Faith and Other Cotton Patch Sermons*,
> Clarence Jordan, page 28. Copyright © 1972 Florence Jordan.
> Used by permission of Association Press and Koinonia Partners.

But the resurrection of Jesus shows us a God who stubbornly refuses to "go back home," a God who will not be told no. In fact, God raised his Son from the dead and sent him again to preach, to teach, and to heal in our midst.

We sometimes think that God raised Jesus from the dead so that we may have a way to get to heaven when we die. But that just isn't so. The primary importance of Jesus' resurrection is not our whereabouts after death but that it speaks about where God is present now. The Resurrection tells us that God now dwells forever *right here on earth*. The risen Christ is not standing on heaven's side of the grave cheerfully motioning to us to join him there. Instead, he joins us in the midst of life here and now. He is right beside us, sustaining us in this life.

The resurrection of Jesus is therefore good news indeed, but not primarily because we get to go home with Jesus when we die. It is good news because the resurrected Jesus has chosen to come home with us. But Jesus does not come alone; he brings with him his brothers and sisters—the hungry ones, the naked, the thirsty, the sick, those in prison—and asks us to care for them (Matthew 25:31-46).

On the morning of the Resurrection, God gave us God's transforming presence. The proof of Jesus' resurrection, then,

> is not the empty tomb, but the full hearts of his transformed disciples. The crowning evidence that he lives is not a vacant grave, but a spirit-filled fellowship. Not a rolled-away stone, but a carried-away church.
>
> From *The Substance of Faith and Other Cotton Patch Sermons*, page 29.

The goal of Jesus' resurrection is to reshape our lives as his followers so that we may begin to live the way Jesus' lived and to think the way Jesus thought. In short, the thrust of the Resurrection is to help us believers change our way of life so that it begins to resemble Jesus' way of life.

For us Christians, the Resurrection is the greatest event in the world. It means that we live all of life in the presence, love, and power of our Lord and Savior, Jesus Christ.

Where will you meet Jesus this week? Where will you experience the living presence of the risen Lord? Where will you discover signs of hope in the places where you live, work, and play each day? How may your daily living be evidence of the power of Jesus' resurrection?

As you begin the third week of this study, think of the places in your community where you might meet God and where your daily living might witness to the power of Jesus' resurrection.

• Opening Prayer •

(Pray this prayer every day as a way to begin your time with God.)

Almighty God, through Jesus Christ you overcame death and opened for us the gate to everlasting life. Grant that we who celebrate the day of our Lord's resurrection may, by the renewing of your Spirit, arise daily from the death of sin to the everlasting life of righteousness. Through Jesus Christ, our Lord. Amen.

• Scripture Readings •

(Read the Scripture for the day slowly and meditatively.)

Day 1 John 20:1-8   **Day 5** Acts 10:34-43

Day 2 Luke 24:1-35   **Day 6** Romans 8:31-39

Day 3 Mark 16:1-8   **Day 7** 1 Corinthians 15:1-11

Day 4 Matthew 28:1-10

• Prayer of Formation •

(Pray this prayer to examine your life before God and to be formed in the faith. Pray the prayer below, then add to it your thanks to God for this day and for family and friends. Pray for your church family. If you are using this guide as part of a group, pray for the other participants. After the prayer, proceed to Readings for Reflection.)

Lord, make me an instrument of thy peace;
where there is hatred, let me sow love;
where there is injury, pardon;
where there is doubt, faith;
where there is despair, hope;
where there is darkness, light;
and where there is sadness, joy.

O Divine Master,
grant that I may not so much seek
to be consoled as to console;
to be understood, as to understand;
to be loved, as to love;
for it is in giving that we receive,
it is in pardoning that we are pardoned,
and it is in dying that we are born to eternal life.

Francis of Assisi, Italy, 13th century

• Readings for Reflection •

(Read one or more of the following readings prayerfully each day. As you meditate, look for connections among the readings, the Scripture passage for the day, and the prayers.)

He is Lord, he is Lord!
He is risen from the dead and he is Lord!
Every knee shall bow, every tongue confess
that Jesus Christ is Lord.

—Tom Fettke, "He Is Lord" (Philippians 2:9-11)

The resurrection of Jesus is not a spectacular event with crashing cymbals and blaring trumpets. No, the discovery that He is alive is like the quiet dawning of a new day heralding the defeat of the night. The risen Christ meets His friends personally and intimately at unexpected times and places, overcoming their grief and doubt. They are flooded with joy and peace as they move from sight to faith.

—Roger L. Fredrikson, *The Communicator's Commentary: John*

This is a day of new beginnings,
time to remember and move on,
time to believe what love is bringing,
laying to rest the pain that's gone.

For by the life and death of Jesus,
God's mighty Spirit, now as then,

can make for us a world of difference,
as faith and hope are born again.

Then let us, with the Spirit's daring,
step from the past and leave behind
our disappointment, guilt, and grieving,
seeking new paths, and sure to find.

Christ is alive, and goes before us
to show and share what love can do.
This is a day of new beginnings;
our God is making all things new.

—Brian Wren, from "This Is a Day of New Beginnings"

The disciples...wanted Jesus with them, wanted him nearby in case questions needed answering, in case wounds needed healing; they wanted him where they could lean on him, and follow his lead, and altogether bask in his presence. They had a Lord they could see, and hear, and touch, and they liked it that way. Oh, and wouldn't we like it too—a God with skin, with a smell, with a humanity we could hang on to. Stay with us! Stay, Stay. But he died; he went away, and although several of them saw him later, it was never the same again. "They have taken away my Lord, and I do not know where they have laid him," weeps Mary outside his tomb, and indeed she never sees her Lord again, but sees instead the risen Lord, the death-defying Messiah, so changed that she does not recognize him in the garden, as Simon Peter does not recognize the stranger on the shore, as these two disciples do not recognize the foreigner who joins them on the road to Emmaus. And what chaos it creates, this resurrection of his. Where can the disciples turn now for guidance? Who will tell them what to do next? How can the body of the faithful live without its head, its heart? He comes and goes, walking in through closed doors and out them again, unswayed by their pleas that he stay. Stay with us! Stay. Stay.

But he will not stay, that is the truth of it—not for them and not for us—he will not stay put, stay the same, stay with us. "Stay!" That is our chorus, but his refrain is, "Follow!" *Follow me*, he says over his shoulder as he moves out into the world, broadcasting his Holy Spirit, blending into the crowd of humanity so well that, if we choose to go after him, we must search every face on the off chance that it might be his.

—Barbara Brown Taylor, *Mixed Blessings*

Those are our choices, it seems: we can beg him to stay with us or we can follow him. We can plead with him to stay put and, when he does not, we can sit alone with our memories and perhaps even make some up—whatever will fuel our nostalgia and grief, which are all we will have left. We can do that or we can go after him, plunge into the crowd right behind him and, although the sea of faces that parted for him closes back in on us, still we can catch a glimpse of him here and there, in the face of a gardener, a foreigner, a stranger on the road. If we are thorough we will handle each person we meet with care just in case it is he; if we are diligent we will wash some feet along the way, feed some hungers, soothe some sorrows, just in case they are his. You can never be too sure.

Of course, the problem with this approach is that we are likely to forget exactly what he looked like. With so many faces to sort through, some of the details are likely to get lost. Were his eyes brown, or a faded blue like that old woman's? Was his complexion smooth, or wrinkled like that weary-looking fellow's? Did he walk straight, or a little stooped, like that boy with the crutch? Chances are, that in looking for him and wanting so much to find him, that we will begin to see a little bit of him in everyone we meet. So the problem with this approach is that the whole human race may begin to bear a family resemblance to the one we seek, so that when he walks up to us in his completeness we do not recognize him. Or at least not at first.

—Barbara Brown Taylor, *Mixed Blessings*

The Skin Horse had lived longer in the nursery than any of the others. He was so old that his brown coat was bald in patches and showed the seams underneath, and most of the hairs in his tail had been pulled out to string bead necklaces. He was wise, for he had seen a long succession of mechanical toys arrive to boast and swagger, and by-and-by break their mainsprings and pass away, and he knew that they were only toys, and would never turn into anything else. For nursery magic is very strange and wonderful, and only those playthings that are old and wise and experienced like the Skin Horse understand all about it.

"What is REAL?" asked the [Velveteen] Rabbit one day, when they were lying side by side near the nursery fender, before Nana came to tidy the room. "Does it mean having things that buzz inside you and a stick-out handle?"

"Real isn't how you are made," said the Skin Horse. "It's a thing that happens to you. When a child loves you for a long, long time, not just to play with, but REALLY loves you, then you become Real."

"Does it hurt?" asked the Rabbit.

"Sometimes," said the Skin Horse, for he was always truthful. "When you are Real you don't mind being hurt."

"Does it happen all at once, like being wound up," he asked, "or bit by bit?"

"It doesn't happen all at once," said the Skin Horse. "You become. It takes a long time. That's why it doesn't often happen to people who break easily, or have sharp edges, or who have to be carefully kept. Generally, by the time you are Real, most of your hair has been loved off, and your eyes drop out and you get loose in the joints and very shabby. But these things don't matter at all, because once you are Real you can't be ugly, except to people who don't understand."

—Margery Williams, *The Velveteen Rabbit*

[Think about the two travelers on the road to Emmaus.] The problem with our two heavy-hearted friends was not a lack of faith, but a lack of vision. Their petitions were limited to what they could imagine—an earthly kingdom. Had God answered their prayer, had he granted their hope, the Seven-Day War would have started two thousand years earlier and Jesus would have spent the next forty years training his apostles to be cabinet members....

We are not much different than burdened travelers, are we? We roll in the mud of self-pity in the very shadow of the cross. We piously ask for his will and then have the audacity to pout if everything doesn't go our way....

Our problem is not so much that God doesn't give us what we hope for as it is that we don't know the right thing for which to hope....

Hope is not what you expect; it is what you would never dream. It is a wild, improbable tale with a pinch-me-I'm-dreaming ending. It's Abraham adjusting his bifocals so he can see not his grandson, but his son. It's Moses standing in the promised land not with Aaron or Miriam at his side, but with Elijah and the transfigured Christ. It's Zechariah left speechless at the sight of his wife Elizabeth, gray-headed and pregnant. And it is the two Emmaus-bound pilgrims reaching out to take a piece of bread only to see that the hands from which it is offered are pierced.

Hope is not a granted wish or a favor performed; no, it is far greater than that. It is a zany, unpredictable dependence on a God who loves to surprise us out of our socks and be there in the flesh to see our reaction.

—Max Lucado, *God Came Near*

Excerpted from the book *God Came Near*, by Max Lucado; Multnomah Publishers, Inc.; copyright © 1987 by Max Lucado.

This risen Christ is with us in the midst of our sinfulness. He takes us just as we are and transforms us into all that we can be. He takes us in the midst of our sin and says, "Go and sin no more."

To paraphrase John Wesley, it takes as great a miracle to bring a man or a woman out of the tomb of sin as to bring Christ's body from the tomb of death. If the Jesus who lived and walked and talked on this earth, who forgave sin, who was crucified and died on the cross is the same Jesus who was raised from the dead, then forgiveness of sin is just as real today as in his day.

—Timothy L. Bias

When the poor ones who have nothing share with strangers,
when the thirsty water give unto us all,
when the crippled in their weakness strengthen others,
then we know that God still goes that road with us,
then we know that God still goes that road with us.

When at last all those who suffer find their comfort,
when they hope though even hope seems hopelessness,
when we love though hate at times seems all around us,
then we know that God still goes that road with us,
then we know that God still goes that road with us.

When our joy fills up our cup to overflowing,
when our lips can speak no words other than true,
when we know that love for simple things is better,
then we know that God still goes that road with us,
then we know that God still goes that road with us.

When our homes are filled with goodness in abundance,
when we learn how to make peace instead of war,
when each stranger that we meet is called a neighbor,
then we know that God still goes that road with us,
then we know that God still goes that road with us

—J.A. Oliver and Miguel Manzano, "Cuando El Pobre (When the Poor Ones)"

Let's...go to the cemetery of our past to look for the Lord of the living. Let's remember Jesus' promise, "If the Son makes you free, you shall be free indeed" (John 8:36). The past can be described as the "if onlys" of our lives. The past is gone and we cannot retrieve it, but much comes out of that past to haunt us. If only I had had parents that loved me more. If only I had studied harder and made more of my life. If only I had chosen a different career. If only I had married that other person. If only I hadn't married. If only my children had not disappointed me. If only I had children. If only my child had lived. We may want to have a resurrection experience over past addictions—alcohol, drugs, self-pity, fear, destructive attitudes. We can leave those "if onlys" in the cemetery and ask the risen Lord to set us free from those crippling memories.

—Bruce Larson, *The Communicator's Commentary: Luke*

In a little United Methodist church in the Midwest, there was a custom where everyone came into the sanctuary after Sunday school to review their Sunday school lesson. The Sunday school superintendent would ask someone in the congregation to stand and review the lesson.

One Sunday the superintendent asked a twelve-year-old girl to review the lesson. She stood and spoke to the congregation, "Our Sunday school lesson this morning was about Enoch and about how Enoch walked with God. Our Scripture was, 'Enoch walked with God; then he was no more, because God took him.'"

The girl went on to explain, "Enoch and God were best friends. Every morning when Enoch got up to walk through the community, God walked with him. Every place Enoch went, God went, because Enoch and God were really close. But about Enoch's death—here's how it happened. Enoch and God were out walking one day, and on their way to Enoch's house it got dark and God said to Enoch, 'I don't think we are going to make it to your house before dark.' And Enoch said, 'That's okay. We are closer to your house anyway. Let's just go and spend the night at your house.' So Enoch went to spend the night at God's house."

She ended the story by saying, "Enoch and God were so close that it didn't make any difference to either one of them whether they spent the night at Enoch's house or at God's house."

—Timothy L. Bias

I was talking…with a friend…about death and the damnation of not knowing what will happen to us. He has lost several dear friends in recent summers—men his age, mostly, who have died in a number of bizarre ways: one from a cerebral hemorrhage on his way home from a lecture tour, one from a heart attack while jogging and one, inexplicably, from a sudden lightning bolt while fishing with his family. My friend worries, of course, that he will be next, and while he worries he keeps remembering a scene from his boyhood in a southern town, how he used to traipse down to the river with some of the older boys and watch them swing far out over the fast-moving water on a rope tied to the branch of a tree. He sat and watched them arc across the sky and then let go of the rope, falling down the air and disappearing into the current. A little ways downstream their heads broke the surface and they swam back to shore, egging him on, urging him to take a turn in the air.

He was afraid, but decided to try; they were his friends, after all, and he had watched them do it. So he decided to do it too. He grasped the rope, got a running start, and swung far out over the water. At the height of his ride he willed his hands to let go of the rope but they would not—it was so far, the water was so fast, he was so afraid. He had watched how the other boys did it, but he had not a clue what allowed them to let go of the rope. So he hung there, dangling between sky and the river, until someone hauled him back to earth.

I do not know how many tries it took him before he finally let go, but he said that when he finally did, it was because of his friends. "They had all gone ahead of me," he said. "I had watched each of them let go and finally I just made up my mind that if they could do it I could do it too—without knowing what would happen, without knowing whether I would make it or how it would be—I just opened my hands and let go, because I wanted to join those who had gone ahead of me." He remembers that episode, he says, because that is what it is like now, watching his friends die. Still afraid of letting go, he has watched each of them do it and believes more and more that maybe, just maybe, when it is his turn he can do it too, if only because they have gone ahead of him.

Fine, you may say, that is a very nice story, but there is one very important difference: those boys swam back to shore to tell him everything would be all right. Who has come back across the river of death to tell us the same thing? It all depends on whom you believe, and if you believe. There was…Jesus, who faced his own death with great uncertainty and fear but who was willing to let go, to step out into the air without a net. Some said they saw him later and that he talked about peace, about how it had turned out there was nothing to fear after all, and that the water was fine. It all depends on whom we believe, and if we believe. It all depends on whether, when it is our turn, we can let go of the rope, let go of our illusions of control, let go of our fears and step out into whatever God-given, death-defying mystery comes next.

—Barbara Brown Taylor, *Mixed Blessings*

Because he lives, I can face tomorrow;
because he lives, all fear is gone;
because I know he holds the future,
and life is worth the living just because he lives.

—William J. and Gloria Gaither, from "Because He Lives"

• Suggestions for Reflection and Action •

(As you read, pray, and reflect each day, write your thoughts, feelings, and reflections under "Your Thoughts for the Week," page 46. The questions below may help focus your meditation.)

- What is God saying to me through the Scripture reading, prayers, and readings for reflection?
- Where are there signs of hope in the community?
- Where do I experience God in the places where I live, work, and play?
- How can God be present to others through me?
- How can God be present to the community through my congregation?
- What one action of faithful discipleship am I going to take today?

• Closing Prayer •

(Pray this prayer to close your time with God.)

O God, help me to be aware of your presence in every situation I am in today. Give me ears to hear what you are saying. Give me a heart and mind to discern and understand what you are doing in the world. Make me a blessing to someone today. Amen.

• Your Thoughts for the Week •

(Use this page as a personal record of your journey with God. Write your thoughts, feelings, insights, and prayer concerns daily as you reflect on the Scripture reading, prayers, readings for reflection, Suggestions for Reflection and Action questions, and your own daily living.)

The Spirit of Jesus

INTRODUCTION

HAVE YOU EVER NOTICED how important breath is? Some of the old television commercials really tried hard to get us to notice with lines like, "I just ate onions, kiss me," or "While the Joneses are sleeping, a dingy film collects in their mouths." And when the alarm clock sounds the next morning, Mr. and Mrs. Jones put their hands over their mouths and mumble self-consciously, "Mornin'." Thank goodness for the toothpaste that promises a fresh mouth and sexy breath! In our North American culture, breath—at least clean breath—is very important.

It is true: breath is very important. In fact, breath is a matter of life and death. I remember playing army with some friends as a little boy. Upon "shooting" somebody we would watch his or her stomach to see if it moved. If the stomach moved, it meant that the person was not "dead." So we would shoot the person again to make sure. Breath is a matter of life and death.

Breath is a matter of life and death in the Bible, too. The Hebrew word for spirit, *ruach*, is also the word for breath or wind. God breathed into Adam the breath of life (Genesis 2:7). Ezekiel uses *ruach* in his account of the valley of dry bones (Ezekiel 37:1-14). He writes, "Thus says the Lord GOD: Come from the four winds, O breath, and breathe upon these slain, that they may live." Whereupon the foot bone connected to the ankle bone, the ankle bone to the leg bone, and the leg bone to the knee bone until all the dead bones had risen and were dancing. Indeed, there is life in the midst of death.

In the New Testament, the Greek word for spirit means breath or wind. In John's Gospel, Jesus appears to the disciples after his resurrection, breathes on them, and says, "Receive the Holy Spirit" (John 20:22). For John, the Holy Spirit is Christ's living presence.

Spirit receives a somewhat different emphasis by Luke, both in his Gospel and in the Acts of the Apostles. After the crucifixion of Jesus, everyone assumed not only that Jesus was dead but also that the whole movement associated with him was dead. The church was dead before it really got started! Even though Easter had come and there was a glimmer of hope, many people considered the Resurrection an idle tale.

Only a handful of people were convinced that Jesus was alive. Those who believed were barely hanging on to hope. Then they encountered the resurrected Jesus in Jerusalem and heard the Lord say to them, "John baptized with water, but you will be baptized with the Holy Spirit not many days from now. ...You will receive power when the Holy Spirit has come upon you; and you will be my witnesses in Jerusalem, in all Judea and Samaria, and to the ends of the earth" (Acts 1:5, 8).

These few followers took Jesus seriously. They shut themselves up in a little room. Even though they were frightened and disillusioned and discouraged, they prayed. Day after day passed; they continued to pray. Nothing happened. But they continued to pray. The sick remained sick. The blind did not receive sight. The lepers were still diseased. The helpless still needed help, as did those who cried for comfort. But Jesus' faithful followers continued to pray. Meanwhile, there were no new converts. The church seemed lifeless, like a tomb. With Jesus gone, what hope was left? The Jesus movement seemed finished; and Jesus' followers looked like fools. What was left for them to do? Only pray—and so they did. They locked themselves in the upper room and they prayed.

And then in the midst of their praying, Scripture tells us, "Suddenly from heaven there came a sound like the rush of a violent wind, and it filled the entire house where they were sitting" (Acts 2:2). It was a mighty activity—not some soft, gentle breeze but a force of power. That is Luke's understanding of the Spirit: the Spirit is God's power. The Spirit's power filled the whole house. The Holy Spirit, the breath of God, transformed those tired, disillusioned, discouraged disciples into a powerhouse—into God's church. And the Spirit transformed not just the pulpit but the pews. Not just the congregation but the community. Not just the community but the whole world.

Where will you meet Jesus this week? Where will you experience the power of God's Holy Spirit? How will you be empowered by the Holy Spirit to be the disciple God has created you to be? How will those around you be empowered by the Holy Spirit to live as Christ's disciples?

As you begin the last week of this study, think of the places in your community where you might meet God and where the Holy Spirit might empower you in your everyday living.

• Opening Prayer •

(Pray this prayer every day as a way to begin your time with God.)

> Spirit of the living God, fall afresh on me.
> Spirit of the living God, fall afresh on me.
> Melt me, mold me, fill me, use me.
> Spirit of the living God, fall afresh on me.

> "Spirit of the Living God," by Daniel Iverson. © 1985 Birdwing Music
> (ASCAP). All rights administered by EMI Christian Music Publishing.
> International Copyright Secured. All Rights Reserved. Used By Permission.

• Scripture Readings •

(Read the Scripture for the day slowly and meditatively.)

Day 1	Acts 2:1-47	**Day 5**	1 Corinthians 12:4-31
Day 2	John 16:4-15	**Day 6**	1 Corinthians 13:1-13
Day 3	John 20:19-23	**Day 7**	Galatians 5:22–6:10
Day 4	Ephesians 4:1-13		

• Prayer of Formation •

(Pray this prayer to examine your life before God and to be formed in the faith. Pray the prayer below, then add to it your thanks to God for this day and for family and friends. Pray for your church family. If you are using this guide as part of a group, pray for the other participants. After the prayer, proceed to Readings for Reflection.)

> Lord, make me an instrument of thy peace;
> where there is hatred, let me sow love;
> where there is injury, pardon;
> where there is doubt, faith;
> where there is despair, hope;
> where there is darkness, light;
> and where there is sadness, joy.

O Divine Master,
grant that I may not so much seek
to be consoled as to console;
to be understood, as to understand;
to be loved, as to love;
for it is in giving that we receive,
it is in pardoning that we are pardoned,
and it is in dying that we are born to eternal life.

Francis of Assisi, Italy, 13th century

• Readings for Reflection •

(Read one or more of the following readings prayerfully each day. As you meditate, look for connections among the readings, the Scripture passage for the day, and the prayers.)

O Great Spirit,
whose breath gives life to the world,
and whose voice is heard in the soft breeze:
We need your strength and wisdom.
Cause us to walk in beauty. Give us eyes
ever to behold the red and purple sunset.
Make us wise so that we may understand
what you have taught us.
Help us learn the lessons you have hidden
in every leaf and rock.
Make us always ready to come to you
with clean hands and steady eyes,
so when life fades, like the fading sunset,
our spirits may come to you without shame. Amen.

—Traditional Native American prayer

When we are living, it is in Christ Jesus,
and when we're dying, it is in the Lord.
Both in our living and in our dying,
we belong to God, we belong to God.

Through all our living, we our fruits must give.
Good works of service are for offering.
When we are giving, or when receiving,
we belong to God, we belong to God.

'Mid times of sorrow and in times of pain,
when sensing beauty or in love's embrace,
whether we suffer, or sing rejoicing,
we belong to God, we belong to God.

Across this wide world, we shall always find
those who are crying with no peace of mind,
but when we help them, or when we feed them,
we belong to God, we belong to God.

—Roberta Escamilla (Stanzas 2, 3, 4), "Pues Si Vivimos (When We Are Living)"

In December 1983, eleven-year-old Trevor Ferrell saw a television news report on Philadelphia's inner-city homeless. The young boy couldn't believe people actually lived on the streets. When he questioned his parents, Frank and Janet reluctantly agreed to broaden their son's sheltered horizons—and their own. They left their home in an exclusive suburb and drove downtown.

A block past city hall, they spotted an emaciated figure crumpled on a sidewalk grate. While his parents watched a bit apprehensively, Trevor got out of the car and approached the man.

"Sir," he said, "here's a blanket for you." The man stared up at Trevor at first. Then, "Thank you," he said softly. "God bless you."

That encounter altered the Ferrells' lives forever. Night after night they drove downtown, trying in small ways to help the street people. They emptied their home of extra blankets, clothing, and dozens of peanut-butter sandwiches. When others learned what they were doing, someone donated a van and volunteers charted nightly food distribution routes. To the Ferrells' surprise, "Trevor's Campaign" had begun.

Young Trevor found himself explaining what they were doing to local media, then to the nation. Pat Robertson, Merv Griffin, Mother Teresa, Ronald Reagan—all wanted to meet the small boy with the big mission. He told them simply, "It's Jesus inside of me that makes me want to do this."

But Trevor is a reluctant celebrity. He endures interviews with one eye on the door. He doesn't know why people make such a fuss over him. Is it because helping the homeless is so unusual? In that case, says his father, the more who follow Trevor's example, the better.

"Our social life has changed a lot since the campaign began," Frank says. "Our church is behind us one hundred percent; but some of our old friends don't understand why we're messing with the homeless. They just tolerate our 'eccentricities.'"

Nightly now, the blue van travels the downtown streets of Philadelphia. It stops first to deliver food to the residents of Trevor's Place, a ramshackle rooming house where some of the formerly homeless now live. Then it proceeds to feed the hungry people gathered on sidewalk grates and street corners.

Asked how these handouts can make a difference in the complex business of helping the homeless, Frank Ferrell sighs. "We're trying to meet short-term needs and figure out ways to bring long-term changes to these people's lives. Sometimes it seems like just a band-aid. But this is how we build relationships. These people become our friends, and they trust us to help them in bigger ways."

Frank pauses for a moment, looking at the landscape of broken bottles and bodies. "There are plenty of struggles. But I know one thing: giving has made all the difference in my Christian life. I used to just read the Scriptures. Now I feel like I'm living them."

—Charles Colson, *Kingdoms in Conflict*

Every time I feel the Spirit
moving in my heart, I will pray.
Yes, every time I feel the Spirit
moving in my heart, I will pray.

—From "Every Time I Feel the Spirit"

Afro-American spiritual (Romans 8:15-17)

Lord, I want to be more holy in my heart. Here is the citadel of all my desiring, where my hopes are born and all the deep resolutions of my spirit take wings. In this center, my fears are nourished and all my hates are nurtured. Here my loves are cherished and all the deep hungers of my spirit are honored without quivering and without shock. In my heart above all else, let Thy love and integrity envelop me until my love is perfected and the last vestige of my desiring is no longer in conflict with Thy Spirit. Lord, I want to be more holy in my heart.

—Howard Thurman, *Meditations of the Heart*

Teach us, our Father, that if we nourish within our minds and spirits those things that work against life, we shall spend our years stumbling in the darkness; that if we nourish within our minds and spirits those things that make for life, for wholeness, for truth, for love, we shall become like Thee. To become like Thee, O God, our Father, is the be-all and end-all of our desiring.

—Howard Thurman, *The Growing Edge*

Howard Thurman, *The Growing Edge*, paperback ed., Richmond, Ind.: Friends United Press, 1974, p. 61.

Evangelism is witness. It is one beggar telling another beggar where to get food. The Christian does not offer out of his bounty. He has no bounty. He is simply guest at his Master's table and, as evangelist, he calls others too.

—Daniel T. Niles, *That They May Have Life*

Copyright © 1951 by The Student Volunteer Movement for Christian Missions. Copyright renewed. Used by permission of HarperCollins Publishers, Inc.

Together, you and God are a majority. I'm reminded of an NBA rookie who played on the Chicago Bulls team in the prime of superstar Michael Jordan. During one particular game Jordan went wild and scored a magnificent sixty-eight points. The rookie rode the bench until the last minute of the game, when the coach graciously sent him in. He made a single free throw during the final seconds of the contest. When interviewed in the post-game show, the rookie was very pleased with himself. "Together," he said, "Michael Jordan and I scored sixty-nine points."

—Dr. James Dobson, *Life on the Edge*

Life on the Edge, Dr. James Dobson, © 1995 by James Dobson. Used by permission of Word Publishers, Nashville, TN. All rights reserved.

I play a little tennis—not much, but a little. I want you to imagine that I've been playing with my friend and pastor, Larry Hall, every Saturday for two years. And every Saturday he's been waxing me regularly, beating me soundly. Then, in some mysterious way, I find that I can receive the tennis ability of John McEnroe. And so I do, but nobody knows it except me, and I look the same on the outside.

So the next Saturday, we're on the court ready to play and ol' Larry's standing there saying to himself, "Oh boy, my patsy is here. I'm going to feel good this afternoon after I've beaten him again." Then he says out loud, "You serve, Miller. It's okay." (Because he knows he can return my serve—right down my throat.)

I just can't wait to serve. So I toss up the ball and hit it, and he doesn't even see it. He looks at me and says to himself, "It looks like Keith Miller, but it serves like John McEnroe."

It's a fanciful, right-brain story, but the Bible indicates that, with the Holy Spirit in my life, I have the power to love with the effectiveness of Jesus Christ himself (see John 14:12-14). The mind's mine, the body's mine, but the spirit is the Spirit of God—when I have been converted and filled with the Holy Spirit.

—Keith Miller, *The Scent of Love*

Write thy blessed name, O Lord, upon my heart, there to remain so indelibly engraven, that no prosperity, no adversity shall ever move me from thy love. Be thou to me a strong tower of defence, a comforter in tribulation, a deliverer in distress, a very present help in trouble, and a guide to heaven through the many temptations and dangers of this life.

—Thomas à Kempis, 14th–15th centuries

Change my heart, O God,
make it ever true;
Change my heart, O God,
may I be like You.

You are the Potter,
I am the clay;
Mold me and make me,
this is what I pray.

Change my heart, O God,
make it ever true;
Change my heart, O God,
may I be like You.

—Eddie Espinosa, "Change My Heart, O God"

A Jewish couple were arguing over the name to give their firstborn. They finally asked the rabbi to come and intercede.

"What is the problem?" the rabbi asked.

The wife spoke first. "He wants to name the boy after his father, and I want to name the boy after my father."

"What is your father's name?" he asked the man.

"Joseph."

"And what is your father's name?" he asked the woman.

"Joseph."

The rabbi was stunned. "So, what is the problem?"

It was the wife who spoke again. "His father was a horse thief, and mine was a righteous man. How can I know my son is named after my father and not his?"

The rabbi thought and then replied, "Call the boy Joseph. Then see if he is a horse thief or a righteous man. You will know which father's name he wears."

To call yourself a child of God is one thing. To be called a child of God by those who watch your life is another thing altogether. [You will be known by the fruit you produce.]

—Max Lucado, *A Gentle Thunder: Hearing God Through the Storm*

Do you want your life to make a difference in this world? Then produce "Son-ripened" fruit:

"Love	Patience	Faithfulness
Joy	Kindness	Gentleness
Peace	Generosity	Self-control

...There is no law against such things....If we live by the Spirit, let us also be guided by the Spirit" (Galatians 5:22-25).

—Timothy L. Bias

This friend and I were in graduate school together. He went on to teach at Trenton State University....[The friend, Charlie, eventually got tired of pouring out his heart every day teaching, then having to endure the pain of comments such as, "Do we have to know this for the final?" He felt like he died a little with each lecture. So he quit, went back to his hometown, and became a mailman.]

Later his mother telephoned me and said, "Tony, you have to go and talk to

Charlie. He quit his job. He's a Ph.D. in English literature and if he doesn't teach, what can he possibly do?"...

So I hunted him up [and talked with him about his decision]....And it wasn't long before I realized that I couldn't dissuade him from his decision to give up teaching....I couldn't change his mind, so I came back with the old Protestant work ethic thing. I said, "Charlie, if you're gonna be a mailman, be the best mailman you can be."

He looked at me with a silly grin and said, "I'm a lousy mailman....Everybody else gets the mail delivered by one o'clock, I never get back until about five-thirty or six."

"What takes you so long?" I wanted to know.

He said, "I visit! That's why it takes so long. You wouldn't believe how many people on my route never got visited until I became the mailman. But I've got this problem, I can't sleep at nights."

I asked, "Why can't you sleep?"

He said, "Who can sleep after drinking twenty cups of coffee?"

I began to get the image of this mailman on the job. He was no ordinary mailman. I could picture him going from door to door and at each home giving more than the mail. I could see him visiting solitary widows, counseling troubled teenagers, joking with lonely old men. I could see him delivering the mail in a way that was revolutionary for the people on his route.

He's the only mailman I know that on his birthday, the people on his route get together, hire out a gym, and throw a party for him. They love him because he's a mailman who expresses the love of Jesus everywhere he goes. In his own subtle way, my friend Charlie is changing his world, changing the lives of people, touching them where they are, making a difference in their lives.

[For most of us, when we receive power to be witnesses, we are asked to go home. We are asked to deliver the mail as Jesus would deliver the mail, to wash the dishes as Jesus would wash the dishes, to talk with people the way Jesus would talk with people, to work with people the way Jesus would work with people. Jesus said, "You are my witnesses." We are agents of God working in the redemption and the transformation of the world, beginning in the places where we live, work, and play.]

—Tony Campolo, *You Can Make a Difference*

Breathe on me, Breath of God,
fill me with life anew,
that I may love what thou dost love,
and do what thou wouldst do.

Breathe on me, Breath of God,
until my heart is pure,
until with thee I will one will,
to do and to endure.

Breathe on me, Breath of God,
till I am wholly thine,
till all this earthly part of me
glows with thy fire divine.

Breathe on me, Breath of God,
so shall I never die,
but live with thee the perfect life
of thine eternity.

—Edwin Hatch, "Breathe on Me, Breath of God"

• Suggestions for Reflection and Action •

(As you read, pray, and reflect each day, write your thoughts, feelings, and reflections under "Your Thoughts for the Week," page 58. The questions below may help focus your meditation.)

- What is God saying to me through the Scripture reading, prayers, and readings for reflection?
- Where are people empowered to be disciples in the community?
- Where do I experience God in the places where I live, work, and play?
- How can God be present to others through me?
- How can God be present to the community through my congregation?
- What one action of faithful discipleship am I going to take today?

• Closing Prayer •

(Pray this prayer to close your time with God.)

O God, help me to be aware of your presence in every situation I am in today. Give me ears to hear what you are saying. Give me a heart and mind to discern and understand what you are doing in the world. Make me a blessing to someone today. Amen.

• Your Thoughts for the Week •

(Use this page as a personal record of your journey with God. Write your thoughts, feelings, insights, and prayer concerns daily as you reflect on the Scripture reading, prayers, readings for reflection, Suggestions for Reflection and Action questions, and your own daily living.)

Using *Emmanuel!* for Group Study

INTRODUCTION

JOHN WESLEY BELIEVED that "Christian conferencing" was a means of grace for Christians. By Christian conferencing he meant Christians sharing their experiences and understanding in deliberate and serious conversation. He designed the "class meeting" to enable Christians to gather to learn from one another. Such a fellowship of Christian conversation and shared life ignites love for one another and sparks fresh insight into God's Word.

Using *Emmanuel!* in a small group over a period of four weeks can be a true means of grace. The material in this appendix helps the leader to guide the group in experiences of Christian conversation and learning—that is, in "Christian conferencing."

Let's begin with some basic questions about designing a successful group experience:

How many sessions are there and how long should each take?

We recommend that the group meet for a total of five sessions: an initial session to orient participants to the study, followed by four sessions to cover the weekly study material provided in this book.

Each session should last at least one hour. Participants should covenant to attend all sessions if possible.

How do participants prepare for the group sessions?

It is vital to the success of the group's experience that participants read and reflect on the Scripture reading, the prayers, and the readings for reflection daily, as well as reflect on their own experience in relation to these.

To accomplish this, we recommend the following method: Participants always begin Day 1 of their Scripture readings, prayers, and reflections for the week on the day immediately following the group meeting.

For example, if the group meets on Sunday, participants will begin on Monday with Day 1 of their reading and reflection. Day 7 of their reading and reflection will fall on the following Sunday, the same day that participants meet for the next group session. Groups meeting on a day other than Sunday should simply shift the schedule to fit their meeting day.

Who should lead the group sessions?

The entire study may be led by one person, or leadership may be shared among members from week to week. As leader, your task is to

- determine ahead of time how to conduct the group discussion in each session. It may not be possible to use all the prayers and readings for reflection given for a session. Select those prayers and readings that can be discussed most meaningfully in the time available. Make sure all participants are comfortable with your selections. Give them the freedom to add and delete selections as they see fit. The daily Scripture readings should always guide discussion.

- model a style of openness, honesty, and warmth. When directing questions to and eliciting responses from the group, be the first to share, especially when it comes to personal experiences.

- moderate the discussion. Encourage reluctant members to participate, and prevent any one person or small group from dominating the discussion.

- keep the conversation centered in participants' personal faith experiences of Christ rather than in academic debate.

- honor the time schedule. If it is necessary to exceed the agreed-upon time frame for the session, pause to obtain the group's consensus to extend the meeting time by fifteen or thirty minutes in order to complete the session.

- see that everyone knows the time and place for all sessions, especially if the group meets in different homes. If meetings are held in the church building, the setting should be informal and comfortable. If meetings are held in one or more homes, the host or hostess should minimize interruptions as much as possible.

- make sure that the meeting room is prepared ahead of time and that materials needed for the sessions are available (see "Preparation for the Sessions," below).

Preparation for the Sessions

As you prepare for each session, consider these suggestions:

1. Review the purpose for the session, which is to discuss the key event for that session (the birth of Jesus, the crucifixion of Jesus, the resurrection of Jesus, or the Spirit of Jesus) in light of participants' prayerful engagement during the preceding week with the daily Scripture readings, the prayers, the readings for reflection, and their daily living. Read carefully the introductory material for the week, which discusses the meaning of the week's key event. The Introduction sections are found on the following pages in this book: the Birth—pages 9–11; the Crucifixion—pages 23–25; the Resurrection—pages 35–37; and the Spirit—pages 47–49.

2. Prepare the room where the group will meet.

- Make sure that the room is large enough to allow the group to break into small groups. Make sure that the chairs can be easily moved to form one circle for the whole group and several circles for small groups. If the room is too small to accommodate several small groups, make sure that there are additional meeting places for the small groups.

- Arrange for participants who are bringing symbols or visual aids to bring them a few minutes before class. Prepare the display of these items before the group arrives.

- Be sure that the following items are available as needed: pencils; notebook paper; chalkboard and chalk, dry-erase board and markers, or newsprint and felt-tip markers; extra Bibles.

- If the group meets in a member's home, work with the host or hostess to make sure that the above needs are met.

3. As the leader you should faithfully read and reflect upon the Scripture readings, prayers, and readings for reflection for each week. Choose one of the small groups and participate as a member of that group during the fellowship and prayer times.

Suggested Format for Group Sessions

As you think about how to structure and conduct the weekly group sessions, consider this format:

Welcome and Opening Prayer (5 minutes)

After assembling the group, welcome participants and state the purpose for the session: to discuss the key event for the session (the birth of Jesus, the crucifixion of Jesus, the resurrection of Jesus, or the Spirit of Jesus) in light of participants' prayerful engagement during the preceding week with the daily Scripture readings, the prayers, the readings for reflection, and their daily living. Open the session with prayer, or ask another member of the group to do so.

Fellowship (10 minutes)

Have the members form small groups of two or three. Encourage group members to welcome one another and inquire about one another's well-being by asking, "How are you today?" Members who are willing may tell about a time when they experienced God's presence during the past week.

Discussion (30 minutes)

Reassemble the large group and guide participants in a time of "Christian conferencing." Help group members discover connections between their own experience of faith in daily living on the one hand, and their engagement with the key event for the week, the daily Scripture readings, the prayers, the readings for reflection, and their daily living on the other hand.

The following questions may be helpful in guiding discussion:

1. Which of the daily Scripture readings was most helpful or challenging to you?

2. How does this Scripture reading help you understand the key event?

3. How does this Scripture reading speak to the challenges and concerns you face daily?

4. Which reading in the Readings for Reflection was most helpful or challenging to you? Why?

5. Based on your reflection this week on the daily Scripture readings, the prayers, the readings for reflection, and your daily living, what did you learn about your relationship with God, with Christ, with yourself, and with others? What did you learn about your responsibility to God and others?

6. Has your reflection on this week's key event (the birth of Jesus, the crucifixion of Jesus, the resurrection of Jesus, or the Spirit of Jesus) changed the way you live daily? If so, how?

7. If God has come to be with us in Christ, how can we as Christians be with others in the places where we work and live each day?

8. Where in the community can we experience the presence of Christ?

Record, or have someone else record, insights as participants discuss these issues. Be sure to hold before the group the challenge of seeing how these insights may guide the participants' ministry, both as individuals and as a community of faith.

Prayer (10 minutes)

Have the group break into the same small groups of two or three that they formed for the fellowship time. You may want to remind participants that nothing binds a group together more than praying for one another. Encourage each small group to listen to the prayer concerns of each of its members. A question such as, How can I pray for you today and in the coming week? may help members share. Ask that members use this time to pray together for the concerns expressed by each person.

Encourage the participants of each small group to pray for one another every day until they next meet. Remind participants that they will remain with the same small groups for the fellowship and prayer times for all of the sessions. This consistency will help strengthen mutual commitment and accountability.

Reassemble the entire group and close the prayer time with a prayer that thanks God for each person in the group, for the opportunity to learn together about the key events in the life of Christ, and for the opportunity to grow in faith through this group study.

Sending Forth (5 minutes)

Briefly introduce to the whole group the topic for the coming week. Encourage participants to be faithful both in their reading and in their participation in group meetings. Make sure that participants know the time and place for the next session. Invite participants to bring to the next session symbols or visual aids that remind them of the key event to be studied. Ask that participants bring the symbols early so that you can prepare a display of the items before the group arrives.

Close the session with prayer, using either the Closing Prayer found in each session in this book, or your own prayer.

Send the group forth to serve as missionaries in the world, saying something like, "When you leave this room you enter the mission field, where people need a kind, caring, encouraging word. God sends you to live and speak that word in the places where you live, work, and play. God is preparing the people you will meet. God wants to touch them through you. The joy and peace of the Christian life come in sharing what you have already received. In the name of the living God, in the love given to us in Jesus Christ, and in the power of God's Holy Spirit, go in peace to experience the joy of Christian living."

The First Session: Orientation

As noted earlier, we recommend that groups study *Emmanuel!* in five sessions: one session for group orientation and four sessions to reflect on the key events of the birth of Jesus, the crucifixion of Jesus, the resurrection of Jesus, and the Spirit of Jesus. The orientation session is intended to accomplish at least the following aims:

- It allows members of the group to get acquainted with one another. This is important for establishing a non-threatening environment and a covenant of love in which Christian conferencing can take place. Therefore, each participant should introduce himself or herself to the whole group. Titles should be dispensed with; everyone should be on a first-name basis.

- It allows the leader to orient the group to the purpose of *Emmanuel!*, which is to provide a setting in which the group can discuss the key events in the life of Christ in light of participants' prayerful engagement with daily Scripture readings, prayers, readings for reflection, and their own daily living over a period of four weeks. The intent of the group's interaction and reflection is to help everyone gain deeper insight into the meaning of Jesus Christ, and into how to be a faithful follower of Christ in the places where one works, lives, and plays.

- It allows the leader to make sure that everyone has a copy of *Emmanuel!*, and that the group understands and agrees to at least the following: ground rules for group discussion; time and place for group sessions; format for conducting group sessions (see "Suggested Format for Group Sessions," page 62); and how to use *Emmanuel!* daily (see "How to Use This Guide," page 7).

- It allows the leader to encourage the group to prepare for the first study session ("Week One: Emmanuel! The Birth of Jesus") by reflecting daily on a Scripture reading, prayers, and readings for reflection on the birth of Jesus, pages 11–20. The leader may also encourage members to bring to the next session symbols or visual aids reminding them of the Incarnation.

The orientation session is also a good opportunity to divide the large group into groups of two or three for fellowship and prayer (see "Suggested Format for Group Sessions," page 62). Members of the small groups can become acquainted and begin to pray for one another, both in the session and in the week to come.

As leader, bring the orientation session to a close with a message that creates excitement, anticipation, and commitment for the weeks ahead. Close with a prayer that thanks God for each member of the group, for the opportunity to learn about the key events in the life of Christ, and for the opportunity to grow in faithful discipleship.